THE DOMINIE WORLD OF ANIMALS
OTTERS

D1611257

Graham Meadows & Claire Vial

Contents

Dominie Press, Inc.

About Otters

Otters belong to the same family as weasels, skunks, and badgers. Various **species** of otters are found worldwide, except in Australia, New Zealand, and Antarctica. They live in **habitats** ranging from high mountain ranges to low-lying **tropical** forests and oceans. Otters are ideally adapted to life in the water. They have long, slender bodies, webbed feet, and **tapered** tails.

Some scientists say there are nine species of otters, while others say there are as many as thirteen.

Where Otters Live

This book is about two species of otters, sea otters and Oriental small-clawed otters.

Oriental otters are found over much of Southern Asia, from India to China and as far south as Indonesia. They live mainly in rainforests, near streams, rivers, mangrove swamps, and marshes.

Sea otters live in salt water. Some sea otters live in the South Pacific Ocean, off the coast of Argentina.

The Oriental otter spends most of its life on land. The sea otter hardly ever leaves the water.

What Sea Otters Look Like

Sea otters can grow to be about four feet long, and they weigh up to seventy pounds. The fur on a sea otter's head is a lighter color than the fur on its body.

Because they spend almost all their lives in the water, sea otters have a lot of webbing on their hind feet, which they use as flippers. Their front feet have less webbing than their hind feet. Sea otters have claws on all four feet. They can pull in their claws. Sea otters' tails are short and thick. They are shaped like paddles.

People used to hunt sea otters, which are now an **endangered species**.

What Oriental Otters Look Like

Oriental otters are the smallest of all the otter species. They are about two feet long and weigh between six and nine pounds. Their feet are only partially webbed, with less webbing on their front feet than their hind feet.

The Oriental small-clawed otter has been given its name because its claws are very short. The claws on its front feet look more like fingernails than real claws.

How Otters Groom Themselves

Otters spend a lot of time in the water. To keep their fur waterproof, they **groom** themselves regularly. This grooming spreads oil from their skin through their coat. The oil protects their fur from the water.

Sea otters use their front feet to squeeze water from their fur and then blow air into it. They have very thick fur. Unlike other **aquatic** mammals, sea otters have no blubber under their skin to help keep them warm.

Oriental otters groom themselves by nibbling and licking at their fur, and by rolling around on the ground.

What Sea Otters Eat

Sea otters float above beds of kelp, or seaweed, and feed on the animals that live among the kelp. Their **diet** includes sea urchins, crabs, and shellfish such as clams, mussels, limpets, and abalone. Some sea otters catch and eat fish.

Sea otters mainly feed at dawn and dusk. They dive down into the kelp beds and search for their food. They use their front feet to find and catch their **prey**. Sea otters usually dive as deep as twenty or thirty feet below the surface of the water, but sometimes they plunge as deep as 200 feet in search of food.

How Sea Otters Use Tools

Most of the animals that sea otters eat have a hard shell. In order to get at the soft flesh inside the shell, sea otters have learned to use a stone as a tool to break open the shell.

Once a sea otter has found an animal with a shell and returned to the water's surface, it floats on its back with the stone on its chest. Then the otter holds the shell between its front feet and pounds it against the stone until the shell breaks.

Some people think that sea otters have a favorite stone that they carry around with them and use again and again.

What Oriental Otters Eat

Oriental otters usually rest or sleep in a **den**, or holt, during the day and hunt for their food at night. They mainly feed in shallow water, paddling along the surface as they search for food. Their diet includes snails, mussels, crabs, frogs, and fish. When they find a frog or a fish, they react quickly and chase it through the water. They twist and turn through the water, using their tail as a **rudder**.

Oriental otters often travel more than five miles a night.

Otter Families

Oriental otters often form family groups numbering up to fifteen animals. These groups include an adult male and several females and their young.

Sea otters form large groups that float over the kelp beds where their food lives. These groups, called rafts or pods, can contain up to several hundred animals. Each group is made up of either males only, or females with their young.

An Oriental otter group is called a band of otters.

Their Young

Sea otters usually give birth to one baby, or cub, at a time while they are in the water. Their newborn cubs are already well-developed, and their eyes are open. Sea otter cubs weigh about four pounds at birth.

Oriental otters give birth to their cubs on land. The female finds a dry den where it can give birth. The den must be close to a food supply so that the mother otter can feed herself while taking care of her cubs. The female gives birth to between two and six cubs, which are blind and completely helpless. Each cub weighs less than two ounces.

How Young Otters Grow Up

Oriental otter cubs develop slowly. Their eyes open at about five weeks of age. By the time they are ten weeks old, they play outside the den. They don't start to learn to swim until they are about three months old.

Sea otter cubs grow up much faster. At birth they can already float, because they have fluffy, thick fur that is full of trapped air. About six weeks after they are born, they can swim. Not long after that, they can dive under water with their mother.

Otters can live from ten to twenty years.

Glossary

aquatic:	Animals or plants that live in the water
den:	A safe place where a wild animal gives birth, takes shelter, rests, or sleeps
diet:	The food that an animal or a person usually eats
endangered species:	Types of animals that are at risk of disappearing forever
groom:	To clean
habitats:	The places where animals and plants live and grow
prey:	Animals that are hunted and eaten by other animals
rudder:	Something that is used to steer
species:	Types of animals that have something in common
tapered:	Something that is wider at one end than the other
tropical:	Areas that are very warm throughout the year

Index